W9-AXX-299

Other books by Exley:

Art Lover's Quotations
Women's Quotations
Business Quotations

Music Lover's Quotations
Book Lover's Quotations
Garden Lover's Quotations

Published simultaneously in 1993 by Exley Publications in Great Britain, and Exley Giftbooks in the USA

12 11 10 9 8 7 6 5 4 3

Selection and arrangement © Helen Exley 1993.
ISBN 1-85015-432-5

A copy of the CIP data is available from the British Library on request. All rights reserved. No part of this publication may be reproduced or transmitted in any form or by any means, electronic or mechanical, including photocopy, recording or any information storage and retrieval system without permission in writing from the Publisher.

Edited by Helen Exley.
Text research by Margaret Montgomery.
Designed by Pinpoint Design Company.
Picture research by Image Select.
Typeset by Delta, Watford.
Printed and bound in Spain.

Exley Publications Ltd, 16 Chalk Hill, Watford, Herts WD1 4BN, United Kingdom.
Exley Giftbooks, 232 Madison Avenue, Suite 1206, NY 10016, USA.

Acknowledgements: Toni Bentley: extracts from *Winter Season*, published by Random House, Inc; Gerald Jonas: extract from *Dancing*, published by BBC Books at £20 in hardback; Margaret H'Doubler: extracts from *Dance: A Creative Art Experience*, published in 1968 by The University of Wisconsin Press, Wisconsin, USA; Donald Hamilton Fraser: extract from *Dancers*, published by Phaidon Press; Lillian B. Lawler: extract from *The Dance in Ancient Greece,* © 1964 by Lillian B. Lawler, Wesleyan University Press. By permission of University Press of New England; Shirley MacLaine: extracts from *Dancing in the Light.* Copyright © 1985 by Shirley MacLaine. Used by permission of Bantam Books, a division of Bantam Doubleday Dell Publishing Group, Inc; Curt Sachs: extract from *World History of the Dance*, published in 1937 by W.W. Norton & Co Inc; Walter Sorrell: extracts from *Dance in its Time,* copyright © 1981 by Walter Sorrell. Used by permission of Doubleday, a division of Bantam Doubleday Dell Publishing Group, Inc. Picture Credits: Archiv Für Kunst, Berlin, cover and pages: 6, 9, 18, 21, 37, 39, 40, 43, 44, 46, 48, 55, 56, 60/61; Art Resource, pages: 28, 58; Bridgeman Art Library, title page and pages: 11, 12/13, 17, 23, 26, 53; Christies, London, pages: 12/13, 53; E.T. Archive, pages: 35, 50; Fine Art Photographic Library, back cover and page 24; Giraudon Art Library, pages: 30, 32; Heydt Museum, Wuppertal, page 23; Index, page 17; Musée d'Orsay, Paris, cover and page 24; Musée Toulouse-Lautrec, Albi, page 18; Museo de Arte Moderne, Barcelona, page 17; Museum Voor Kunsten, Ghent, page 58; National Gallery of Scotland, page 26; Pushkin Museum, Moscow, page 37; Scala, page 15.

DANCE
Lovers
QUOTATIONS

EDITED BY HELEN EXLEY

EXLEY
NEW YORK • WATFORD, UK

"The fact that there has always been dance compels us to accept it as an old and deeply rooted human activity whose foundations reside in the nature of being human. It will continue as long as the rhythmic flow of energy operates, and until humans cease to respond to the forces of life and the universe. As long as there is life, there will be dance."

MARGARET N. H'DOUBLER

"Man dances. After the activities that secure to primitive peoples the material necessities, food and shelter, the dance comes first. It is the earliest outlet for emotion and the beginning of the arts...."
SHELDON CHENEY

※ ※

"On no occasion in the life of primitive peoples could the dance be dispensed with. Birth, circumcision, and the consecration of maidens, marriage and death, planting and harvest, the celebration of chieftains, hunting, war and feasts, the changes of the moon and sickness - for all of these the dance is needed."
CURT SACHS

※ ※

"Not only did drama as such - the art of which *action* is a pivotal material - arise out of primitive dance... Music, too, which can hardly be dissociated from the theatre's beginnings, traces its ancestry to the sounds made to accentuate the primitive dance rhythm, the stamping of feet and clapping of hands, the shaking of rattles, the beating of drums and sticks. Dance, then, is the great mother of the arts."
SHELDON CHENEY

"**I** feel I was born to dance."
GREGG BURGE

⚘ ⚘

"Every day I count wasted in which there
has been no dancing."
FRIEDRICH NIETZSCHE (1844 - 1900)

⚘ ⚘

"For every prima ballerina assoluta, there are
several dozen members of the corps. But if you
want to dance you don't care if you never even
get to be a cygnet."
JESSE O'NEILL

⚘ ⚘

"A child sings before it speaks, dances almost
before it walks. Music is in our hearts from
the beginning."
PAMELA BROWN, b. 1928

⚘ ⚘

"To dance is to give oneself up to the rhythms of all life."
DR. MAYA V. PATEL, b.1943

᚛᚜

"What is the first thing that we can imagine that each individual experiences. A movement when you're swishing around inside a mummy's tummy and a heartbeat and a pulse and that's why the basic beat is a one beat with an up beat. And a rock 'n' roll and a marching. It is the most basic beat and now baby is born and what happens to baby. Baby goes aagh, aagh and rocks in time. It moves in time and makes a sound in time. It is singing and dancing. That's what it's doing."
JACQUES D'AMBOISE
(Artistic Director, National Dance Institute)

᚛᚜

"To me dance represents life - and because life is a rhythm, that of the heartbeat - dance is inseparable from rhythm. It interprets our existence, to the extent that it represents all the rhythms, all the human pulsations."
MAURICE BÉJART, b. 1927

᚛᚜

"Dancing is as great a mystery as painting or drama. It serves no obvious purpose - yet it is as much a part of human life as food gathering and sleep."
DR. MAYA V. PATEL, b.1943

"In the Middle East, people dance at circumcisions; in Africa, they dance at funerals; in Puerto Rico, they dance at baptisms; and virtually everyone dances at weddings. There are also rites of passage that are not tied to a particular time and place: whenever and wherever young people seek each other out for companionship, music and dancing are almost always part of the scene."
GERALD JONAS

⧊ ⧊

"For the Indian, dance is a personal form of prayer. When the Eagle Dancer puts on his costume, when he begins to dance to the music, he doesn't simply perform it; he actually becomes the eagle itself. The dancer is virtually inseparable from the dance."
JAMAKE HIGHWATER

⧊ ⧊

"So esteemed was dance that it was accepted practice for statesmen, generals, philosophers, and other outstanding Greeks of the Periclean Age to perform solo dances before audiences of many thousands, on important public occasions."
RICHARD KRAUS

"The subject matter of African dance is all-inclusive of every activity between birth and death. The seed which trembles to be born, the first breath of life, the growth, the struggle for existence, the reaching beyond the everyday into the realm of the soul, the glimpsing of the Great Divine, the ecstasy and sorrow which is life, and then the path back to the earth - this is the dance."

PEARL PRIMUS (1919-1994)

"People dance, as they have always danced, to celebrate good news. They dance on state occasions, to honour a guest, pay court to someone powerful, or simply to demonstrate their social standing. They dance to encourage a sporting team and to exhibit the best and most beautiful in their community. They dance to express their individuality, and for physical contact with the opposite sex.... Performed alone, dance is both a physical and emotional form of release. Dance has been used in all these ways for thousands of years."

PETER BUCKMAN,
from *Let's Dance*

❧ ❧

"But if we look for proof, the popularity of dancing can best be judged by the huge literature of its condemnation. Many preachers would claim that dancing resulted in 'uncleane kyssinges, clippynges and other unhonest handelynges'. And there was not one friar or itinerant preacher who would not have depicted dancers as being struck by lightning, consumed by heavenly fire, or cursed to dance until they fell dead."

WALTER SORRELL,
from *Dance In Its Time*

❧ ❧

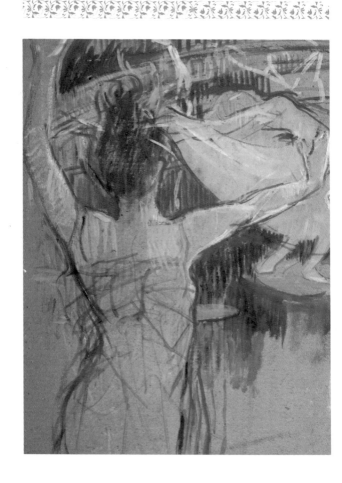

"Ballet is full of mysteries. Take the question of dancers' health. Before company class starts every day at ten o'clock they straggle in, drawn and ashen-faced. How it alarms me. I put it down to their diet of black coffee, chocolate bars and cigarettes. Poor girls, how could they have even managed the stairs let alone survive an hour or two of class. They line the studio with bags and bundles that disgorge a cargo of bandages and woollies, plasters and cotton wool. It is less a dance studio and more a casualty ward as they pad and plaster bruised feet, tie scarves like tourniquets around their heads and waists, heave themselves into plastic trousers - gingerly lest they awaken past injuries. As they hobble about I wonder how these invalids will ever bear the rigours of the barre. Then, against all reason, a daily miracle takes place. As the first notes of the piano are struck, far from wilting they begin to shimmer with well-being. Their eyes open wider, their hair starts to shine, their skin glows and, as the time for centre work arrives the general radiance is dazzling. The miracle is that they are drawing strength from the very act of dancing itself, living off it, and nourished by it. As a long day of rehearsal passes the energy drawn from the dance seems to grow until the accumulated vitality is offered to their evening audience as an incomparable gift."

"We have a different bodily structure than most humans. Our spirits, our souls, our love reside totally in our bodies, in our toes and knees and hips and vertebrae and necks and elbows and fingertips. Our faces are painted on. We draw black lines for eyes, red circles for cheekbones and ovals for a mouth."

TONI BENTLEY

❧ ❧

"...the practice costumes, which included many-coloured pullovers - mostly in a state of disrepair - worn over scant tunics and whatever coloured tights happened to be to hand. The hair was worn back from the ears and kept in place by nets and bandeaux. Ubiquitous thighs were encased in knitted pullovers. Feet, that looked so dainty on the stage, appeared long and bony in darned pink satin ballet shoes. Save possibly in the bosom of a mother, ecstasy is not one of the emotions that is evoked by the spectacle of a dancer working in class."

CARYL BRAHMS AND S. J. SIMON,
from *A Bullet in the Ballet*

❧ ❧

"**I**t [dancing] is an art that imprints on the soul. It is with you every moment, even after you give it up. It is with you every moment of your day and night. It is an art that expresses itself in how you walk, how you eat, how you make love, and how you do nothing. It is the art of the body, and as long as a dancer possesses a body, he or she feels the call of expression in dancer's terms."

SHIRLEY MACLAINE, b. 1934,
from *Dancing in the Light*

❧ ❦

"It is an amazing thing, this ballet. Those who once allow themselves to come within its grasp never escape. The boy and girl who entered the Imperial schools while still children remain as true to it in their old age as ever they were. The great ones, like Fokine, make their last bow while the breath of creation is still fierce in them. It is something that claims its devotees utterly. It makes beauty of the stuff of legends and becomes itself the breeding-place of legends."

GEORGE BORODIN,
from *This Thing Called Ballet*

❧ ❦

"The small child at dancing class may never become a professional dancer - but the courtesies and disciplines, as well as the joy in movement, will touch her forever."
HELEN THOMSON, b.1943

⧟

"To sing well and to dance well is to be well-educated."
PLATO (c. 428 - c. 348 B.C.)

⧟

"A nondescript teacher gives a child the chance to hear applause for the first time, at the local church hall. A good teacher gives a child the ability to hear music with its whole body and to give it visible form."
PAM BROWN, b.1928

⧟

"If all children in every school from their entrance until their graduation ... were given the opportunity to experience dance as a creative art, and if their dancing kept pace with their developing physical, mental, and spiritual needs, the enrichment of their adult life might reach beyond any results we can now contemplate."
MARGARET N. H'DOUBLER

"The value of the dance, its greatest value, is in the 'intangibles'. Success in the dance cannot be measured by a tape, weighed on scales, nor timed with a stopwatch. It demands an awareness and sensitivity in the dancer's soul and in the soul of the beholder who partakes, vicariously, empathetically, in the dance."
TED SHAWN

⚎ ⚎

"All that is important is this one moment in movement. Make the moment important, vital, and worth living. Do not let it slip away unnoticed and unused."
MARTHA GRAHAM (1893 - 1992)

⚎ ⚎

"Dancing is the last word in life ... in dancing one draws nearer to oneself."
JEAN DUBUFFET (1901 - 1985)
(French artist)

⚎ ⚎

"The real reason I dance is because
I want to explode."
BILL EVANS

❧ ❧

"Music is an immediate, emotional, the most powerful
bang. There's a conduit from those vibrations in the
atmosphere that go through the ear, through the mind,
the chemistry through emotions to our heart. But the
same with gestures. Gesture is a communication form
that is in our bones stronger than the content of words
and the meaning of words....
Every time I dance I have a high. I mean every time I
danced, it was the whole world was the stage and I was
in control of it and there was a form and a ritual and yet
it was spontaneous and life didn't matter after that or
before. The whole instant was all the globe in the
universe at the moment. Bang. At that moment. The
exhilaration after would go on constant, still in the
morning and the next day and you're all excited and
yet you never know if you can perform again.
Each performance is your closing night and it's
your opening night."
JACQUES D'AMBOISE
(Director, National Dance Institute)

❧ ❧

"When you perform...you are out of yourself - larger and more potent, more beautiful. You are for minutes heroic. This is power. This is glory on earth. And it is yours nightly."
AGNES DE MILLE

※ ※

"His [the dancer's] body is simply the luminous manifestation of his soul... This is the truly creative dancer, natural but not imitative, speaking in movement out of himself and out of something greater than all selves."
ISADORA DUNCAN (1878 - 1927)

※ ※

"Dancers have a direct connection to the heavens and the gods - Balanchine and Stravinsky receive their talents and visions from God, and we as their instruments interpret those visions for mortal men. We are their servants. We are creative in the same way that the paint in the pot is creative. We are the means to the end. We are essential, and we are on display. We receive the applause. Alone we are incapable and stationary."
TONI BENTLEY

※ ※

"Nothing has ever taken its [ballet's] place for disciplinary training. There is no technique in any other style of dancing that is so valuable for producing exactitude, precision, sense of form and sense of line."
TED SHAWN (1891 - 1972)

❧ ❧

"To enter the School of the Imperial Ballet is to enter a convent whence frivolity is banned, and where merciless discipline reigns."
ANNA PAVLOVA (1881 - 1931)

❧ ❧

"Ballet's image of perfection is fashioned amid a milieu of wracked bodies, fevered imaginations, Balkan intrigue and sulfurous hatreds where anything is likely, and dancers know it."
SHANA ALEXANDER

❧ ❧

"Someone once said to me that dancers work as hard as policemen: always alert, always tense. But you see, policemen don't have to be beautiful at the same time!"
GEORGE BALANCHINE (1904 - 1983)

"The accomplished dancer is an artificial being, an instrument of precision, and he is forced to undergo rigorous daily exercise to avoid lapsing into his original, purely human state.
His whole being becomes imbued with that same unity, that same conformity with its ultimate aim that constitutes the arresting beauty of a finished aeroplane, where every detail, as well as the general effect, expresses one supreme object - that of speed. But where the aeroplane is conceived in a utilitarian sense - the idea of beauty happening to superimpose itself upon it - the constant transfiguration, as you might call it, of the classic dancer from the ordinary to the ideal is the result of a disinterested will for perfection, an unquenchable thirst to surpass himself. Thus it is that an exalted aim transforms his mechanical effort into an aesthetic phenomenon.
You may ask whether I am suggesting that the dancer is a machine? Most certainly - a machine for manufacturing beauty - if it is any way possible to conceive of a machine that in itself is a living, breathing thing, susceptible of the most exquisite emotions."

ANDRÉ LEVINSON,
from *Theatre Arts Anthology, 1950*

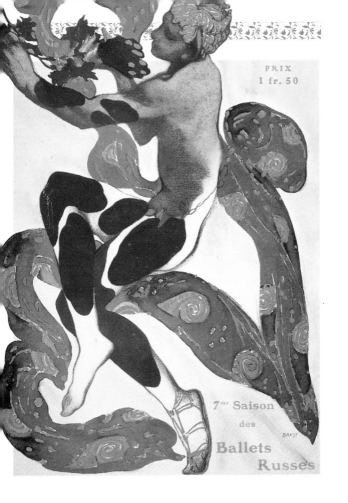

PRIX
1 fr. 50

7me Saison
des
Ballets
Russes

BAKST

"There is fatigue so great that the body cries, even in its sleep. There are times of complete frustration; there are daily small deaths."
MARTHA GRAHAM (1893 - 1992)

※ ※

"Dance can give the inarticulate a voice."
PAMELA BROWN, b.1928

※ ※

"Dancing is a sweat job.... When you're experimenting you have to try so many things before you choose what you want, and you may go days getting nothing but exhaustion. It takes time to get a dance right, to create something memorable."
FRED ASTAIRE (1899 - 1987)

※ ※

"All there is to be said for work as opposed to dancing is that it is so much easier."
HEYWOOD BROUN,
from *Pieces of Hate*

※ ※

"...spectators sometimes sat in the theaters for whole days, watching the dancers almost as if hypnotized; they thought of the dancers as virtually divine, and Seneca calls the craze for their performance 'a disease' - *Morbus*. Women swooned, high officials of the state hung on every move, and Roman emperors summoned the dancers for command performances...."
LILLIAN B. LAWLER, 1964

❧ ❧

"But the people could not help dancing. Since it was a burst of running, skipping, and jumping, disharmonious, it often reached riotous proportions at the threshold of the churches. During the years of the plague such dancing was particularly wild, often reaching a point of hysterical gaiety, as if the people would have liked to trick death or laugh its frightening sight away. In an often cited game they played, someone would suddenly throw himself or herself to the ground and act dead, while the others would dance around in the manner of mock mourning. If it was a man, he would be kissed back to life by the women, whereupon a round dance followed. They were playing 'life and death' like a children's game, with a child's mentality ..."
WALTER SORRELL

❧ ❧

"There was simply from this quite early age the awareness that the only thing I wanted was to dance."
RUDOLF NUREYEV (1939 - 1993)

⚔ ⚔

"When I was younger and I would hear music, no matter what type of music it was, I would start choreographing in my mind.
I would envision I would see people dancing and I thought everyone did this, you know, I didn't realize that this was something that some people do, but the majority of people don't do that. You know, I'd hear music, but no matter what it was, if it was jazz, I'd find myself tapping and listening and seeing little rhythms or if it was ballet, I'd find myself, you know, envisioning a *pas de deux,* you know. The funniest thing as a child, I had my G. I. Joe and I used to make my G. I. Joe dance."
GREGG BURGE

⚔ ⚔

"**D**ance is a song of the body. Either of joy or pain."
MARTHA GRAHAM (1893 - 1992)

⚔ ⚔

"Ballet is not technique, not a way of doing things, but a means of expression that comes perhaps more closely to the inner language of man than any other."
GEORGE BORODIN,
from *This Thing Called Ballet*

⚔ ⚔

"To dance is to express oneself. To dance ballet is to use oneself to express something beyond oneself."
PAMELA BROWN, b.1928

⚔ ⚔

"Her [Martha Graham's] dance purpose is to give physical substance to things felt, to lamentation, to celebration, to hate, to passion, to the experience of 'frontier', to bigotry, to...underlying passions, dreams, fears and tragedies.... to reveal in solid dance architecture the architecture of the inner man."
WALTER TERRY,
from *Martha Graham*

⚔ ⚔

"Then come the lights, lovingly painted from the front of the theater. You realize that every nuance of your face and body will be visible. The pink jells leave your skin with a silky glow. The spotlight following you burns through your eyes. The bumper lights stage right and left add dimensional color to your arms and legs.
You can see absolutely no one in the audience.
It is alienatingly black.
Then you realize it is all up to you. You are a performer. You forget everything you ever learned. You forget the intricate process of technique. You forget your anxieties and your pain. You even forget who you are. You become one with the music, the lights, and the collective spirit of the audience. You know you are there to help uplift them. They want to feel better about themselves and each other.
Then they react. Their generously communal applause means they like you - love you even. They send you energy and you send it back. You participate with each other. And the cycle continues. You leap, soar, turn, extend, and bend. They clap, yell, whistle, stomp, and laugh. You acknowledge their appreciation for what they see and give them more. And so it goes."

SHIRLEY MACLAINE, b. 1934,
from *Dancing in the Light*

"**G**reat artists are people who find the way to be themselves in their art. Any sort of pretension induces mediocrity in art and life alike."
MARGOT FONTEYN (1919 - 1992)

❧ ❧

"The truest expression of a people is in its dances and its music. Bodies never lie."
AGNES DE MILLE

❧ ❧

"I see the dance being used as a means of communication between soul and soul - to express what is too deep, too fine for words."
RUTH ST. DENIS

❧ ❧

"To dance at all is to confront oneself. It is the art of honesty. You are completely exposed when you dance. Your physical health is exposed. Your self-image is exposed. Your psychological health is exposed.... It is impossible to dance out of the side of your mouth. You tell the truth when you dance. If you lie, you hurt yourself."
SHIRLEY MACLAINE, b. 1934

❧ ❧

"For me, dance is a nutrient, you know, it's something that I need, it's something like, you know, the air we breathe, the food we eat.
These are things, these are necessities. These are things that we need for survival. For me, dance is a nutrient. It's my nourishment."
GREGG BURGE

⊰ ⊱

"If we cannot bring ourselves to dance, we become sick. Dancing heals."
MARION C. GARRETTY, b. 1917

⊰ ⊱

"I don't want people who want to dance, I want people who have to dance."
GEORGE BALANCHINE (1904 - 1983)

⊰ ⊱

"Friedrich Nietzsche thought that to grow beyond his ordinariness, man needed that inner lightness which is the lightness of the dancer."
WALTER SORRELL,
from *Dance in its Time*

⊰ ⊱

"**D**ANCE IS FUN! It lifts the spirit, strengthens the
body, and stimulates the mind...."
WAYNE SLEEP, b. 1948

🖘 🖙

"The essence of all art is to have pleasure in
giving pleasure."
MIKHAIL BARYSHNIKOV, b. 1948

🖘 🖙

"To live and to laugh require a reason. But dancing is so close to one's guts that it has no reason and yet it needs none; it's physical, and as a source of good cheer it is endless."
TONI BENTLEY

"When you start dancing and you feel cool, you feel like the whole world belongs to you."
ESTHER BOATENG

"Dance for yourself. If someone else understands, good. If not, no matter. Go right on doing what interests you, and do it until it stops interesting you."
LOUIS HORST

"Fra Angelico believed in a Dantesque manner that dancing, in particular the carole, was the principal pastime in heaven, a *ballo dei angeli*. This was the notion the early Christians had of angels: singing and dancing while encircling the throne of God."
WALTER SORRELL

"**H**uman life is not based on logic, but on music, on dance, on poetry."
HELEN THOMSON, b. 1943

⚑ ⚑

"One should dance because the soul dances. Indeed, when one thinks of it, what are any real things but dances? I mean the only realities - moments of joy, acts of pleasure, deeds of kindness. Even the long silences, the deep quietness of serene souls, are dances; that is why they seem so motionless."
HOLBROOK JACKSON (1874 - 1948)

⚑ ⚑

"...this loftiest, the most moving, the most beautiful of the arts, because it is no mere translation or abstraction from life; it is life itself."
HAVELOCK ELLIS (1859 - 1939),
from *The Dance of Life*, 1923

⚑ ⚑

"It is what I've always wanted to do - to show the laughing, the fun, the appetite, all of it through dance."
MARTHA GRAHAM (1893 - 1992)

⚑ ⚑

"If we seek the real source of the dance, if we go to nature, we find that the dance of the future is the dance of the past, the dance of eternity, and has been and will always be the same."

ISADORA DUNCAN (1878 - 1927),
from *The Dance of the Future*

⚘⚘

"We look at the dance to impart the sensation of living in an affirmation of life, to energize the spectator into keener awareness of the vigor, the mystery, the humor, the variety, and the wonder of life."

MARTHA GRAHAM (1893 - 1992),
from *The American Dance*

⚘⚘

"It's [dance] your pulse, it's your heartbeat, it's your breathing. It's the rhythms of your life. It's the expression in time and movement of happiness and joy and sadness and energy. It's a venting of energy. It's extraordinary, and that's common to all the cultures and it's common to all individuals."

JACQUES D'AMBOISE
(Artistic Director, National Dance Institute)

⚘⚘

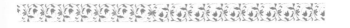

Dance till the stars come down from the rafters;
Dance, dance, dance till you drop.
W. H. AUDEN (1907-1973),
from *Death's Echo*

⚜

"The happiest dance I ever attended was when I found
myself abandoned with a small, plump, teddy bear of a
man. He couldn't dance either.
Suddenly, a wonderful, desperate madness came
over us. Like non-swimmers plunging into a
fast-flowing river, we took to the floor. We had no
idea what we were supposed to be doing, but held
on doggedly and walked in an approximation of the
rhythm in the general direction taken by everyone else.
We 'danced' until we were exhausted."
PAMELA BROWN, b.1928

⚜

On with the dance! let joy be unconfined;
No sleep till morn, when Youth and Pleasure meet
To chase the glowing Hours with flying feet.
LORD BYRON (1788 - 1824)

⚜

"There is a dancer buried in even the fattest of us."
PAMELA BROWN, b.1928

⇄

"If we can think, feel, and move, we can dance."
MARGARET N. H'DOUBLER,
from *Dance: A Creative Art Experience*

⇄

"You can dance anywhere and you can dance in your
mind, in your heart."
JACQUES D'AMBOISE
(Artistic Director, National Dance Institute)

⇄

"There is room in dance for everyone - from walking to
music in someone's arms to the Rose Adagio."
PAMELA BROWN, b.1928

⇄

"And what do you think is your ultimate goal?"
"I should think a nice little dance in heaven."
UNKNOWN DANCER STRUCK DOWN BY POLIO IN 1953

⇄

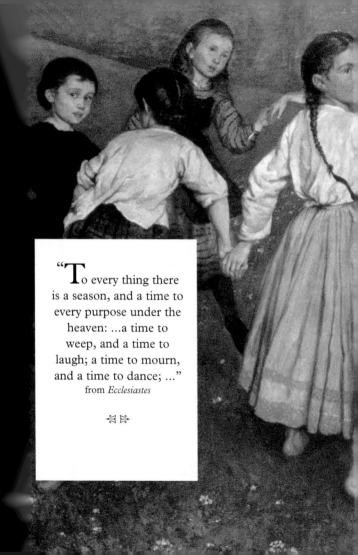

"To every thing there is a season, and a time to every purpose under the heaven: ...a time to weep, and a time to laugh; a time to mourn, and a time to dance; ..."

from *Ecclesiastes*